A Killer Resume

**THE SEVEN SECRET STEPS
TO A RESUME
THAT GETS YOU HIRED EVERY TIME**

Resume Sample Templates Included

Riley Rose

Table of Contents

Introduction

Do you dream about the job you want but have no idea how to write the resume that wins you that interview? Have you applied for countless jobs in cyber space and still have no callbacks or interviews scheduled? Are you in a dead end job and feel your future dwindling away? Are you continuing to get the acknowledging email after each job submission but never hear back from the same company ever again? What happens to your resume after submission? Why isn't it bringing you the opportunity you desperately want or need?

Creating a *killer* professional resume will give you the edge you need to gain access past the scrutinizing gatekeepers who screen your resume and select the candidates' resumes that contains the language they seek. Push back and get out of the unending darkness of your space filled void and find the lighted pathway into professional consideration. You can conquer the stress and dread with the knowledge and desire to shine in your own unique way so the hiring manager or talent specialist chooses your resume out of the pile of applicants all submitting for the same opportunity. Remember to read and follow these guidelines but also to include your unique characteristics so your resume stands out in its own special way.

While both content and layout are important, content is the most significant. Content is the distinction that makes your resume *a killer.*

Included in *A Killer Resume* are several resume templates. You can find many on the Internet for free, in fact. However the content of the resume is what will get you hired.

I became a Certified Professional Resume Writer in 2001. I have written professional resumes for the top three resume writing firms in the United States: resumewriters.com (one of the first resume writing service companies on the Internet), resumeedge.com (began by creating resumes for Ivy League graduates) and militaryresumes.com (for soldiers transitioning from their service careers to government jobs). I have written numerous civilian, military and government specialized resumes. While contracted by ResumeEdge.com and MilitaryResumes.com, I rewrote military resumes for those transitioning into the private marketplace, and/or their transition into government positions. Both military and government resumes are specialized documents that require much detail of respective military and government careers.

I have extensive experience in career counseling and have performed as a successful Executive Recruiter and a Professional Career Consultant, which is demonstrated by my ability to get past the gatekeeper. This recruiting and career consulting experience is a great aid with resume writing. I gained great insight by consulting with many job-seeking clients to get a comprehensive picture of his or her professional background and career objectives. From my consultations, I created complete packages of distinctive marketing tools – writing and editing cover letters, resumes, as well as follow-up and thank-you letters for clients to use in their job search.

My extensive experience in executive recruiting and career counseling has given me the unique insight into the needs and practices of hiring managers across professional disciplines. Knowing what hiring managers are looking for enabled me to create resumes that stood out from the ordinary. Professional resumes and cover letters get results for clients, landing interviews and finding jobs.

For example, my strength at translating business skills and experience into career success led my sales manager, KM, at Wells Fargo Bank to enlist my services. The resume I designed resulted in an offer to set up and run an Accounting and Finance search firm for Ventura County. Another client, PC, was working as an Operations Clerk with Wells Fargo Securities and dreamed of using her degree to attain a coveted position in Human Resources for a Fortune 500 company. Presently (or at the time of writing this book), she is the Senior Vice President of Human Resources for Pepsi and the former Director of Human Resources for Frito Lay in Dallas. She secured the Frito Lay position after working as a Divisional Manager for Human Resources with McKesson HBOC. She attributes the success in her new career to the resume that I wrote for her. She says it gave her the confidence she needed to achieve her ambitions and grab the brass ring. Now she's living and working in her dream job and has the career she had no direction in achieving, when working as a clerk.

Both PC and KM's resumes were badly formatted and clearly not targeted for the jobs they were qualified to have. I rewrote their resumes utilizing the seven secret steps and both acquired their dream positions. KM now runs her own executive search business, consulting for commercial banks and PC has progressively climbed the corporate ladder in the field she desired to work in.

Start searching for the job openings and the career you desire. Don't delay. Presently many candidates submit immediately for hire, so target the job and life you desperately want to lead. Identifying the job description for the job you seek is a big step in the process of designing your professional *killer* resume. Then apply the seven secret steps in this book to write your professional resume and you will have the best marketing tool you need for the job you want.

Chapter 1
Why Do I Need a Professional Resume?

Finding the job you want can be a challenge in today's world of job search. Take a look at LinkedIn's posted job offers; on an average day, several hundred applicants are clicking the same *apply now* button. LinkedIn posts the number of candidates that have clicked the, *apply now,* button for your information. This is why your immediate action is needed. You want to be noticed early in the review process because interviews can start right away and a candidate can be selected while the job search is still in process. You want to be the chosen hire. So your resume needs to be as professional as possible and always unique so that it's *a killer resume.*

Instead of being part of the pack of many, your resume needs to impress the gatekeeper so you can be allowed inside for an interview. Your resume needs to answer the specific questions of targeted experience the employer wants. It has to have a professional presentation and contain the content the resume reviewer seeks. Your resume is your marketing tool that begins the process for acquiring your desired position.

The identified job description will be your reference tool to design the resume that contains the skills as described. Gatekeepers or resume screeners are looking for like language that is contained in the job description so that you are identified as a match for consideration. Having a professional resume that correlates with keywords as described in the job description is what will get you in the consideration pile of applicants.

Below are 12 clear reasons, (part of what I learned from the Professional Association of Resume Writers) for a professional resume:

1.   Site Key Information First – The cover letter and top one-third of a resume must be especially inviting for the reader from both a visual and content point of view. Instead of an Objective, professional resumes should include a Qualifications Summary. This will be covered in the third secret step. The reader must be able to find it easily and weigh it against his or her needs. Remember to follow the guidelines but also include your unique traits so that you are distinct and you are "you". This may be highlighted in design - perhaps you have your own professional logo or a unique volunteer experience to separate you from the pack. However, content is king and what's contained in the resume to satisfy the resume screener and hiring manager is what you seek. This book is your guide for quality resume content.

2.   Choice of Format – Writers use a variety of formats for both resumes and cover letters. There is no such thing as a standardized format. There are subtle differences between the look of an executive resume, a student resume and a blue-collar resume. Student resumes, or people with five years of experience or less, rarely require more than one page. Senior executives or company presidents typically have 2-5 pages or more, and it is not uncommon for a curriculum vita to run as long as 25 pages. However, brevity usually wins out in comparison; one word is better

than two, one page is better than two, two pages are better than three and so on.

3.   Appropriate Words/Phrases/Industry Jargon – Do not confuse slang, which is informal and often colloquial in usage, with keywords and industry acronyms, which are commonly accepted terms that display industry knowledge. Abbreviations are also relative. JD, MBA, CPA, and MD are common business abbreviations that most management-level readers would understand, as well as the dynamics they imply. Industry Jargon, also known as key works, are handy and such phrases can indicate a strong level of sophistication if used properly.

4.   Selection/Accuracy of Data – When writing your resume, you must prioritize large amounts of information. The idea of being complete means that the whole story comes across with maximum impact. Judgment will dictate and should lend to strong interpretation and prioritization of information in handling your given background of experience.

5.   Accomplishments Prominent – Your goal is to create a resume that makes you stand out as a candidate for the job you want. The resume reader should not have to struggle to find what contributions you have made in previous positions. Past performance that is specific to the job description is significant to the employer's point of view.

6.   Proper Context of Data – Briefly put your resume data in proper context wherever possible: succinctly describe the company you worked for in the context of its industry; briefly describe the scope of your responsibilities; use time frames and measureable accomplishments where

applicable and align word choice with status of your level of experience.

7.   Handling of Potential Obstacles – Keep your professional work history to a maximum of 10 years, unless you are a very senior executive and a long work history is expected and required for the position you seek. Typical problems include: a lack of education, returning to the workforce, gaps or short periods of employment. Solutions to these problems must be customized and based on the information as a whole. Instead of a chronological resume, a functional resume might be better. A mixture of functional and chronological resume elements may work for you. See Chapter Seven.

8.   Employer Oriented – Most employers, regardless of their industry, prefer resumes that are reader-friendly. A proper professional format determines typeface (such as Times Roman or Calibri), presents a single or double page length document and is presented on a minimum of a 20-pound bond paper stock (always white in color if mailing or presenting a resume when interviewing). The job description content is a decision that the writer should make from the employer's point of view.

9.   Mechanics – Your resume should be typo and error free with proper number form and usage, punctuation, capitalization, parallelism and proofreading. I suggest avoiding the first or third person usage, instead consider your resume as a newspaper story and report beginning each sentence with an action verb as follows: develops direct-response media campaign for senior management review. You are telling a story, describing your professional career. Make sure each job description is a chronological assessment of your accomplishments you performed at the position you describe.

10.   Organization and Presentation should entail: formatting enhancements – if the job is conservative, the resume should also be conservative; employ formatting consistency; choice of paper and/or print quality; typeface and/or font size; white space; overall readability – meaning how well ideas flow in logical order and how they communicate your marketability to the job description.

11.   Style – should consider: A) creativity/originality – meaning writing in a way you are confident with, as opposed to writing in a way that you think others will find appropriate without overextending the boundaries of effective and professional communication. B) Redundancy and sentence fragments, wherever possible, reinforce the theme of your resume with the cover letter without repeating actual phrases. C) Include interpretation of strengths. D) The initial impressions must be inviting, attractive, and provocative, without being offensive. E) You'll need some command of word processing. F) Be sure to use active verbs and phrases, they bring resumes and cover letters to life. G) Clearness and conciseness are a necessity, don't use any language that leads away from your intended ideas. Your writing should add clarity to your career (story) and its professional message of who you are.

12.   Cover Letter – This is the sales tool for your resume. It should include: A) an opening and a closing, it should pique your resume reader's interest right away and set the tone for what is to follow. It should also be brief; B) the tone should reflect a greater concern for the reader than the client. C) It should have a strong command of language, so write intelligently, with a purpose, and with economy in mind. D) Introduce your resume well, get the attention of your reader by directly addressing their need (or what the

job opening is asking for in terms of skills), explains how you meet the job description needs. Include an element of visualization that allows the reader/screener to see the benefit of interviewing you, which dictates a course of action for follow-up. E) It should be written for the appropriate audience – Human Resource (HR) Managers, Hiring Manager or Senior Executive Staff such as Company Presidents, etc.

Your goal is to get an interview. A professional resume that targets the employer's job description greatly increases your chances of doing that. If you want the right job now, then read this book, apply these, *killer resume,* writing steps and capture the job you want. Read and apply the seven secret steps to writing your professional resume and you will have the marketing tool you want for your new professional *killer resume.*

Remember your well-written resume is the ticket to the job you desperately want. It's your marketing strategy to nail down the career you have targeted and when you land it, it's a wonderful goal to have met.

I have a long list of satisfied clients who've used my services to achieve their career goals. For example; many, like my client FW, emailed me and told me they not only received the promotion they were seeking, but that my materials gave them a significant boost in confidence in their skills and experience.

Versatility is also key. As you write each of your resumes for the different jobs you seek, take note of the tone of the job description - it will aid in your communication of fitting into the professional career world you desire. This was always my goal with the candidates I wrote resumes for and according to Frank Fox, Executive Director of the

Professional Association of Resume Writers & Career Coaches, who reviewed several of my resume examples for my resume writing certification, he gave me the following feedback showing my writing adaptability. His comments were as follows: *"Great looking samples! Each has a different look, which demonstrates your versatility."*

The next chapter begins the first secret step. You will learn why a resume objective is outdated and nonspecific to the particular job you want. Turn the page and begin the professional path to the professional career you want and deserve.

Chapter 2
What's the First Secret Step?

A resume begins with determining the job you want. Your resume is your most powerful marketing element. You must write it to target the exact job description you are applying for. Job descriptions are like cooking by a recipe to prepare your favorite meal. They are your road map to designing your best personal brand.

My great aunt was an excellent cook and a baker. She always taught me to hand select the ingredients I used when I baked a pie or a cake. You should write your resume as if you are writing to the individual that wrote the job description. Although in most cases, you're writing to a recruiter or a screener who may or may not have any specific knowledge about the job you seek but they are still responsible for finding qualified candidates. So they screen by the content description of the job description that you are applying for.

Selecting the correct applicants can be a tedious and overwhelming challenge. I recently spoke to a Search Engine Optimization (SEO) hiring manager, who told me he ran an advertisement for a writer and received 400 resumes in two hours. The response was so large that he was unable to review all of the applicants because of time constraints and his need to hire right away. Once he found a

suitable applicant, he scheduled an interview and
hired his writer quickly.

What was the SEO hiring manager looking for? He looked
for a resume that contained the skills and keywords he
needed in order to do the job. Was the hired candidate the
best qualified for the position? Probably not, however the
writer was experienced and his resume did identify him as
someone who could competently do the job this hiring
manager needed and so he chose the best professional
resume he received within the first hour's pool of
applicants.

Next it is imperative that you have a strong grasp of your
job skills. Each of your job skills will correspond to a
keyword descriptor. These should be utilized throughout
your resume but definitely in the Qualifications Summary
of your resume. Keywords are one to two word descriptors
and/or adjectives that identify your areas of work expertise.
These should come from your professional background of
experience and should correspond to the content in the job
description. You are targeting a job description by utilizing
the correct job skills stated in the description.

Job skills are personal abilities and talents that help
employees carry out work-related tasks. Job skills are
aptitudes acquired by work experience that make a person
valuable to other employers. Many job-related skills are
somewhat broad, including good communication, word
processing and problem solving. Depending on the sort of
work at issue, skills can be very nuanced. Construction
workers need a unique set of abilities different from
lawyers, doctors, or teachers for instance. Many job
announcements set out the skills required for the work and
job seekers also typically list their relevant qualifications in
their application materials.

Some of the most important job skills come second nature to employees. The ability to listen well, to take and apply instructions and to maintain focus for long periods of time are critical to success in almost any workplace. Basic phone courtesy and computer and e-mail skills also fall in this category.

Most of the time, these sorts of skills are assumed: that is, employers expect employees to have them, even if they do not ever say so directly. Job advertisements and openings typically presume a basic level of proficiency when it comes to the basic skills needed to carry out the job. Employees can learn a great many things once they have gotten started, but they usually need to have at least some foundation from which to begin.

In the below resume sample, a keyword section is included beneath the statement of qualifications. The keyword section is derived from this candidate's job skills. This is a method that I often utilize in professional resumes. It adds impact to the candidate's skills, showing clearly that this candidate is directly qualified to fill the job description below.

See the below job description and the corresponding Qualifications Summary of a professional resume sample below.

Job Description:

Senior Change Management Consultant
Job Location: City, State

A pharmaceutical company in City is in need of a Senior Change Management Consultant on a temporary basis.

Interface with a wide range of managers and cross-functional departments. Provide strategic and tactical Organizational Change Management support on a large compliance initiative within client (Serialization) to drive understanding and commitment to business process and system changes leading up to implementation and beyond. Person is responsible for adhering to our client's standards for Organizational Change Management. Duties include but are not limited to assessing impact of change events and readiness to implement, identifying issues, and developing strategy and implementation plan for communications and other Change Management deliverables.

If you have the above qualifications, please email your resume to recruiteremail@recruiteremail.com today! Job ID: 123456789

Qualifications Summary of a Professional Resume:

SENIOR CHANGE MANAGEMENT EXECUTIVE

Organizational Development ~ Compliance Leadership ~ Risk Management

Exceptional leadership demonstrated by managing large staffs in Fortune 500 and multi-million dollar corporations. Trusted presidential advisor of measurement and analysis on all corporate objectives. Extraordinary tactical insight demonstrated in all contract negotiations and corporate legal matters. Expert ability for staff inspired excellence through effective hands-on management and governing abilities. State Bar licensing in California, New York and Nevada. Member of the National Legal Committee for the American Association of Homes and Services for the Aged; Alumni Board of Directors, Stanford University; Alumna Leadership of Los Angeles Community Trust Association; American Bar Association Leader for the National Officer Law Division and House of Delegates Representative. Additional abilities in:

♦ Change Management	♦ Human Resource Ethics	♦ Risk & Cost Analysis
♦ Legal Expert	♦ Training & Development	♦ Business Development
♦ Six Figure Settlements	♦ Recruitment & Retention	♦ Strategic Alliances

The headline of the above resume: "Senior Change Management Executive" also corresponds to the job description title: "Senior Change Management Consultant". Make sure you are qualified to fulfill this responsibility of course, why else would you be applying for this position unless you can competently do the work. Remember you are making these choices because you are applying to be chosen because your skills match the job description's requirements.

Chapter 3
What's the Second Secret Step?

The second secret step is a resume headline. This is the first attention-grabbing element of your most important marketing tool, your resume. The resume headlines are several expressive statements that briefly and creatively highlight key skills and accomplishments throughout your career. These few statements must capture the reader's attention.

The heading or title of a job description is the job title that an applicant should target. Examples include the following: Senior IT Project Manager, Vice President of Insurance, Management Consultant, Head Teacher, etc.

Remember the job description and resume sample below from the previous chapter?

Job Description:

Senior Change Management Consultant
Job Location: City, State

A pharmaceutical company in City name, is in need of a Senior Change Management Consultant on a temporary basis. Interface with a wide range of managers and cross-functional departments. Provide strategic and tactical Organizational Change Management support on a large compliance initiative within client (Serialization) to drive understanding and commitment to business process and system changes leading up to implementation and beyond. Person is responsible for adhering to our client's standards for Organizational Change Management. Duties include but are not limited to assessing impact of change events and readiness to implement, identifying issues, and developing strategy and implementation plan for communications and other Change Management deliverables.

If you have the above qualifications, please email your resume to recruiteremail@recruiteremail.com today! Job ID: 123456789

Here is a Qualifications Summary Sample of a Professional Resume:

SENIORCHANGEMANAGEMENTEXECUTIVE

Organizational Development ~ Compliance Leadership ~ Risk Management

Exceptional leadership demonstrated by managing large staffs in Fortune 500 and multi-million dollar corporations. Trusted presidential advisor of measurement and analysis on all corporate objectives. Extraordinary tactical insight demonstrated in all contract negotiations and corporate legal matters. Expert ability for staff inspired excellence through effective hands-on management and governing abilities. State Bar licensing in California, New York and Nevada. Member of the National Legal Committee for the American Association of Homes and Services for the Aged; Alumni Board of Directors, Stanford University; Alumna Leadership of Los Angeles Community Trust Association; American Bar Association Leader for the National Officer Law Division and House of Delegates Representative. Additional abilities in:

♦ Change Management	♦ Human Resource Ethics	♦ Risk & Cost Analysis
♦ Legal Expert	♦ Training & Development	♦ Business Development
♦ Six Figure Settlements	♦ Recruitment & Retention	♦ Strategic Alliances

This resume's headline is clearly written to attract the attention of the human resource professional screening for qualified applicants to fill the identified job description. The job description title is: "Senior Change Management Consultant" and the resume headline is: "Senior Change Management Executive". This candidate is clearly identified as a qualified applicant for the job title being offered.

A resume headline offers a job seeker the opportunity to shine. A well-formed headline will get your resume placed on top of the pile not stuffed somewhere in the middle. Of course the rest of your resume should also be written well and targeted to the specifics of the job description. The headline adds to a well-formatted and designed resume. A headline is the one component that immediately crabs the recruiters and job screener's attention. Headline targets are flexible and should cater to the company you query. Use a resume headline to make that employer notice you.

Examples of Resume Headlines

Here are some good resume headline samples that you can personalize according to your needs:

- Marketing Campaign Manager
- Corporate Communications Professional
- Professional Account Executive
- Director of Sales
- Sales Manager
- Interior Designer
- Business Developer Professional
- Software Developer
- Research & Development Team Leader

Typically resume screeners spend about 30 seconds on a resume because of the hundreds of resumes they receive for a posted position. Separating yourself from the pack of applicants means a well-designed, professional resume, which communicates that you are an exceptional professional, well qualified to fill the job title being offered. A resume headline communicates this to the screener so your resume doesn't end up in the dreaded circular file – the trashcan.

Chapter 4
What's the Third Secret Step?

Professional resumes should contain a summary statement and not a job objective. A statement tells what qualifies you to fill the job description you are applying for versus a career objective, which tells an employer what you're looking for. To be quite frank, the job recruiter is only interested in the candidates whose background matches the job description they're screening against. Your career objective is therefore unimportant to their candidate search. In fact, most hiring managers recommend that job applicants begin their resume with a resume profile instead of an objective.

What is a resume profile or summary statement? The Professional Association of Resume Writers (PARW) basically describes a career profile as a brief summary of you as an applicant presenting your skills, experiences, and goals as they relate to the specific job opening. A resume objective only states the type of position you are seeking.

Essentially, a profile is a very condensed version of a cover letter. A resume profile is a career summary or personal profile statement, compiled into a summary of qualifications. It profiles your key qualifications for the job you seek.

What are the Benefits of Using a Profile?

Your resume profile that contains a summary of qualifications will stand out among the hundreds of resumes that companies receive for each open position. Presently the job market is very tight and a professional distinction such as a profile statement is vital to the professional presentation of your resume. Why is a profile statement so vital? Most recruiters or gatekeepers evaluating job applicant resumes, spend only a few seconds looking at a resume. Even more importantly, the majority of this time is spent looking at the top half of a resume. Therefore, even if employers only scan your profile (located directly beneath your heading and contact information), they will still have a very clear idea of your unique qualifications.

In addition, your resume profile should include keywords that help your application get picked up by the recruiting management software that many companies use to screen applications for job openings.

Resume Profile vs. Resume Objective

Most employers and headhunters prefer resume profiles to resume objectives. The profile is a paragraph of career statements most applicable to the job description you are applying for. It should include significant accomplishments including your work experience, skills, level of position and qualifications for the job for which you are applying.

While an objective on your resume is a way to convince employers that you know what you want in a job, a profile is specifically more impressive to the hiring manager because it explains what you have to offer the employer and can help sell your candidacy.

Alternatively, less experienced job applicants, such as students right out of high school or college can simply start their resume with their most recent work experience.

For example, while an objective might state, "Experienced Math teacher seeks position at an independent high school," a profile might state, "Math instructor with ten years of experience in public and private school systems. Developed creative teaching strategies and practices that are proven in helping students achieve passing grade levels on statewide assessment exams." Unlike the objective, this profile answers the hiring manager's question, "What can this applicant offer me as the employer?"

What are the Tips for Writing a Resume Profile?

Keep Your Profile Concise. Its length should be between one and four (brief) sentences long. You can write it as a short paragraph or in bullet form.

Each resume should focus on the Job Listing. In your profile statement, only include the skills and qualifications that relate to the specific job for which you are applying. Your profile is particularly helpful if you have work history that is unrelated to your current career goals – it allows you to highlight only your most relevant experience. Each position applied for, should have a profile statement written specifically to apply for its description of requirements and duties.

Consider a resume focus on the future. A profile serves to show what you have to offer an employer; this is what you will do for the company's future growth pattern. Look at the job listing as well as the company's website, news articles or mission statement on the website's 'About' page, for insights into what the company is looking for in an employee. In your profile, explain how you will meet the company's expectations. Does a sales director position require someone who can improve the company's sales conversion record? Your profile may state you are an "accomplished director of sales with success in developing strategies that have generated six- and seven-figure revenue growth." Explain in measureable statements what you have done as a way of showing the hiring manager what you will do in the future: "Ranked #1 out of 10 sales territories, and sited for attaining chairman's club status."

Your resume statement summary is listed where an employer can see it when they first review your resume; so list your profile at the top of the page, above your work history. See the Resume Template Samples at the end of this book or check out: *A Killer Resume*, Table of Contents.

Why Your Resume Profile Statement Gets You Hired

Succinctly standing out is key. Like many hiring managers in the United States, several years back I was faced with a common scenario, a stack of 200 resumes to review for a single job opening (in this case, an entry-level Custody Services Officer).

First, the statistics you hear are true, and according to the Professional Association of Resume Writers and Career Coaches, you really do only have about 30 seconds to make an impression with your resume. As I quickly scanned the resume of an applicant named Jessica, things were looking good. She had held jobs that were relevant to the position, she had a strong educational background, and I sensed from her cover letter that she wanted a professional banking position where she could prove herself. Then I saw the final item on this resume:

Interests: Volunteer for San Francisco Children's Hospital, Fiction Book Club, Tennis, Intermediate Skier and Accredited Pilot

Her interests were a strong fit for the position. The department worked in teams and Tennis can be a strong partner collaboration sport, as well as custody assignments. Alternatively, customer networking to bring in business requires an individual drive, which is clearly demonstrated by her status as an Intermediate Skier and an Accredited Pilot. I was convinced that she would have no problem sourcing contacts for clients, which is a desirous quality for the job position she was seeking.

After a long day of sifting through many, many resumes, this made me smile and I upgraded her from the "Yes/Maybe" pile into the "Bring her in for an interview" pile.

Tennis, Intermediate Skier and Accredited Pilot

Upon meeting her in person, my instincts were correct. She excelled at the standard interview questions, was a strong fit for the position and attacked her job with delight and focus. She folded right in to her team and immediately brought in new bank clients to the group. She was a strong hire, which added value to the team and the department.

So what about when I asked her about her diverse interests? She responded:

"I began flying while in college and am still certified to this day. Tennis, I've played since I was 10 years old. I placed third in my high school state competition and I've love to ski since grade school and presently ski Tahoe regularly. Staying active in these sports and interests requires intense discipline and hard work, the same skills I will bring to this job. I also love to read and really enjoy my volunteer work with children."

I asked, "How did you get involved with the San Francisco Children's Hospital?"

She replied, "Well, I wanted to make a difference but what surprised me was how the kids made a difference in me."

Diverse or Strange Can Also Be Good

I read about a hiring manager who once hired someone that had alligator wrestling on their resume, along with bodybuilding, ice hockey and ballroom dancing. When the candidate was asked about his interest, he said he was a fitness trainer and an enthused competitor of sports. He got into the ballroom dancing with his fiancé and always wanted to wrestle an alligator, so he put it under interests. He was also hired, and turned out to be a strong asset in his new position.

Should everyone have diverse or strange hobbies on their resume? No. But here's what I am saying:

First, 90% of this young man's resume and his interview is what got him the Network Administrator job, but the last 1% got the hiring manager's attention.

What works for an early-stage startup looking to blend technical skills and a fun culture (as in this case) might not fly for the Custody Services Professional bank position.

Know that you're taking a chance with the person looking at your resume. Will they view this strange interest as clever or immature?

What is currently true is that in a sea of competitiveness, you have to find a way to stand out from the many applicants. After all, what is a resume except a collection of statements or bullet points all categorized nicely under job headings or sectioned categories?

As you progress throughout your career, your goal should be to accumulate the best possible profile summary or bullet points under each category. So, where does the summary come from? Try these tips listed below.

Tips - Include Specific Numbers

When looking at resumes, the mistake most often made is not having enough measureable accomplishments under Work Experience. Sometimes it's just a matter of adding the numbers in.

For Example: "Guided over yearly offsite training courses for team members," is rewritten as follows:

"Guided over $250,000 training program for 10 offsite courses for 400 team members."

Sometimes you need to figure out how to go out and grab the numbers you need on your resume. Pretend it's your company that's working on a new iPhone app, and you're looking to get some mobile operating experience on your resume. If you're not currently involved, don't just wait for an opportunity to happen. Volunteer to help out the team in any way you can, through marketing, design, promotion, or other skills. You might not get paid overtime to do it. You might have to put in extra work time or work late for a several months. You might not even get the recognition that the primary team members receive.

Here's the point, you're doing this extra work for a crucial profile statement of a noted bullet point on your resume:

A sample accomplishment statement in mobile might read: Worked on newly-formed emerging media team to help market and promote Time Warner Corporation's premier mobile app, which was downloaded 50,000+ times in the first 15 days and has driven $150,000 in revenue.

Tips - Include Special Skills

What skills are most relevant in your industry? More significant, if everyone in your peer group has the same skills, what complementary skills will set you apart? Whether you're right out of school, newly entering the workforce, a baby-boomer trying to stay current, or a drama major getting into the world of graphic design, there are specific skills that can stand out on your resume.

Of course, some profile statements or bullets take longer than others to achieve. Becoming a published author is hard earned and takes many years and effort to attain. On the other hand, becoming a self-published author with a positively reviewed and best-selling children's e-book on Amazon might take several months and hold the same type of credibility that you are looking for within your niche: web design, Final Cut Pro, HTML, CSS, SEO or CRM software. These are all valuable keywords on your resume that sets you apart from your competition.

Tips - Include Awards, Accomplishments and Achievements

Seek out the career awards in your industry. Included in this search should be your own company's or department's award of stellar work achievement. Some of these accreditations may be competitive, but often the competition pool is smaller than anticipated especially in your own work place.

You will make an impression by declaring your desire for Top Salesperson or Chairman's Club Rank with your manager at the beginning of the year and achieving it will give you that title/award on your resume going forward. Even if you fall short, 1st, 2nd or 3rd runner up or the top 10% of staff isn't a bad accomplishment on your resume either.

Tips - Include Relevant Coursework

Education is changing. Having a top accredited college like Harvard or Yale on your resume will certainly give you an advantage against your competition. However, there is an explosion of online learning sites, which allows you to take courses on almost any topic – even including ones taught at Ivy League schools.

So while you might not have a degree from Dartmouth, Brown or Stanford, demonstrating your ability to keep your skills current and relevant will set you apart. This is critical for workers who graduated from college more than 10 years ago. They are able to demonstrate that their skills are up to date by taking online, evening, or certificate courses in relevant areas.

Important to Show Some Areas of Interests on Your Resume

The most challenging aspect of our present economy is the competitive nature of job search. Usually, the corporate recruiter or hiring manager is selecting candidates from a pool of applicants that have comparable work experience or skills. Taking into account that generally employees spend the majority of their workdays and workweek with their co-workers rather than their families - what makes sense is to consider the intangibles when putting together a work team.

Consider whom you'd like to work with from an equally qualified pool of job applicants. Would you choose someone who has engaging in outside interests like wine collecting, world traveling or a community volunteer?

Translating Outside Interests into Money

Outside interests can accentuate your skills (or keywords on a resume). They can also give you additional contacts for business leads. Building on active outside club membership, community volunteerism or skilled group interests breeds an additional level on business idea exchange and trust to build on with your applicable client database.

Utilizing original avenues of building business demonstrates initiative and a desire to excel in one's job. This can be extremely helpful during job reviews and bonus awards. Remember to emphasize your outside interest skills - they can be useful during job negotiation especially pertaining to a possible increased rank upon your hire.

Outside interests can add distinction to your job search aiding your consideration of increased rank and a higher negotiated salary specifically because of these skills. You have an increased perceived value.

Make a list of your unique interests and add them onto your resume carefully. Make them sound attractive and inviting in a professional world.

Salary Issue

After your professional resume has gotten you an interview and finally a job offer, now comes time to negotiate. Predetermining your salary objectives is critical.

Do some research and find out what the market place pays someone at your rank for the position you seek. If you have market work experience, you'll have some idea. You can network as well with others in your field to predetermine a range given work experience and related advanced education qualifiers. Your third source for salary information is the Internet. Do a search by title and add the keyword *salary* to it. You'll get a varied group of job definitions and locations. Make sure the market is comparable to the location you will be working in. Lastly check www.salary.com, plug in the job title, work experience and location, it will give you an appropriate range to negotiate from.

Chapter 5
What's the Fourth Secret Step?

Most Organizations use recruitment management software to screen candidates for jobs. Instead of a recruiter or hiring manager reviewing your resume, the software screens your resume based on the terms or description content included in your resume. Thus, resume keywords are the words that gatekeepers and/or hiring managers search for in their new database of resumes. In order for your resume to be found, it needs to contain keywords that directly target the job description you are applying for.

Your resume's keywords should include the specific job descriptions you are applying for as well as your skills, software and technology competencies, relevant credentials and previous employers.

For example, based on experience, a candidate for an employee change management position might use the following resume keywords: human resource ethics, recruitment and retention, legal expert as well as risk and cost analysis. A customer service account executive could include: lead conversion, client tracking system, Microsoft Office computer skills and perhaps order entry experience.

The best way to locate keywords for your resume is to utilize a job search engine like: Monster, CareerBuilder or Indeed, there are many to search for job listings with. Review the results to find common keywords listed in the job postings. Incorporate those into your resume. Also check the list for action keywords you can use to describe your skills.

Resume Keywords

Remember most companies use recruiting software to screen candidates for job openings. The resume keywords you should include in your resume should be the words that those hiring managers search for when going through their database of resumes.

Before you start work on your resume, review free resume samples that fit a variety of employment situations. You can find them by doing an Internet search for free resume samples with the job title included in your web engine search. These resumes examples and templates provide job seekers with examples of resume formats that will work for almost every job seeker.

Cover Letter Keywords

Remember to also include more of the job description keywords to describe your skills in your cover letter to increase your chances of getting selected for an interview. This way, if your cover letter is screened, you will have a better chance of getting selected for an interview as a qualified candidate.

Below are Some Resume and Cover Letter Alphabetical Action Verbs. The Professional Association of Resume Writers provides them and well as having used most of them in the resumes I have written since 2001.

Alphabetical Action Verb List

A

Acquired, acted, aided, assembled, achieved, authorized, assessed, assisted, appraised, amended, accomplished, adapted, addressed, analyzed, authored, advised, allocated, altered, accelerated.

B

Balanced, budgeted, built.

C

Commissioned, communicated, coordinated, calculated, compiled, combined, challenged, chaired, committed, contributed.

D

Developed, disclosed, documented, discovered, determined, demonstrated, deferred, distributed, decided, designed, directed, devoted, drafted, doubled, diversified.

E

Eliminated, exchanged, ended, exempted, endorsed, engineered, employed, edited, evaluated, entertained, exercised, expected, earned, elected, engaged, entered, expedited, experienced, enforced, explained.

F

Fueled, figured, fit, formed, facilitated, focused, financed, fortified, functioned.

G

Garnered, granted, generated, guided, grouped, gave.

H

Handled, hired.

I

Implemented, incurred, innovated, improved, identified, installed, inspired, interpreted, instilled, inaugurated, informed, induced interviewed, issued, invested, illustrated, inspected, invented.

J

Jolted, judged.

L

Litigated, lobbied, led, located, lectured, launched.

M

Measured, moderated, motivated, maximized, moved, mediated, multiplied, marketed, mastered, managed, merchandised, modified, met, minimized, modeled.

N

Navigated, negotiated, noticed, narrowed.

O

Observed, oversaw, operated, obtained, oriented, owned, organized.

P

Processed, promoted, planned, performed, pioneered, participated, printed, prioritized, provided, purchased, placed, permitted, profiled, polled, presented, proposed, pursued, persuaded, perceived, preserved, passed, procured.

Q

Quarried, quoted, qualified.

R

Remedied, redesigned, recruited, recovered, ranked, resolved, received, rewarded, revised, revitalized, revamped, responded, recorded, reduced, replaced, retained, retrieved, reversed, ran, raised, reached, restored, rejected, reinforced, reinstated, rehabilitated.

S

Standardized, steered, stimulated, strategized, surveyed, saved, secured, sold, staged, supported, supplied, substantiated, supervised, stabilized, scheduled, screened, settled, separated, sent, selected, shaped, shortened, showed, signed, simplified.

T

Transformed, tested, targeted, trained, tabulated, took, traveled, transferred, tailored.

U

Updated, utilized, uncovered, undertook, unified, united.

V

Visited, verified, validated, valued.

W

Worked, weighed, wrote, witnessed, won, welcomed.

Chapter 6
What is the Fifth Secret Step?

The fifth secret step is a section on Career Accomplishments. Dig deep for resume accomplishments, these are critical and distinctive as discussed earlier in outside interests for your reference.

Often times we underestimate our achievements. In school and at home, we're told not to boast, that modesty is the best policy. Fast forward to adulthood, we show up to our jobs each day and invariably we will do great things, so isn't that enough?

Unfortunately, it's not if you want your resume to get noticed. Employers look for stellar achievers, they want the best candidates who go way above and beyond just their job duties. Your resume gives you an opportunity to describe your best accomplishments just so employers want to take a chance on hiring you.

If you think you have no career accomplishments, reconsider because everybody has them. You just need to identify them pinpointing what they are.

What is the Definition of an Accomplishment?

For your resume, an accomplishment is a description or an example of how you contributed toward your job. It's an achievement that states or describes the type of worker you are. The best employer accomplishments are measurable. See examples 1, 2 and 3 below:

1). A studio tax manager conveys her hands-on accounting prowess: "Reviews divisional submission for quarterly and year-end tax provision; directs and coordinates varying domestic operations projects and assists with inquiries from taxing authorities."

2). A recent college graduate describes her work at a major retail store, training new hires on how to operate a cash register for shoppers during their purchase checkout: "Trains new employees on the POS registers with 100% efficiency and less than a 2% error rating."

3). A structural engineer describes his work for an architectural design firm: "Filled in as a structural drafter when necessary, generated and revised structural details and originated structural plans, elevations and sections."

The Qualifications section of your resume is an optional customized section that lists key achievements, skills, traits, and experience directly relevant to the position for which you are applying.

The Qualifications section, also known as a Career Highlights, Career Summary or Career Profile section, focuses on your specific, relevant experience and explains to the prospective employer that you have taken the time to create a resume that shows how you are qualified for the job you seek.

How do I Identify My Accomplishments?

Set a timer for 10 minutes. Jot down your accomplishments for your most recent position. Write down any contribution award or achievement you can remember, even if it seems minor. Do this exercise for each job position on your resume. To help jog your memory, here are some questions to ask yourself:

1) What are you known throughout your department/company for in terms of how you work or close business?
2) Have you received praise or recognition from your manager or colleagues? In what way (e.g., completing projects ahead of deadline, calming down irate customers, saving money)?
3) Did you receive a promotion, award or commendations from customers or clients?
4) Were you selected for special projects, committees or task forces?
5) Now name three accomplishments that make you proud. Did you complete a particularly challenging assignment? Participate in a solution that improved customer service, enhanced efficiency, saved money/time or increased revenues?
6) If you quit your job, what would everybody say about your work at your good-bye party?

How to Put It All Together?

Since you've completed the accomplishment exercise, now turn your accomplishments into high-impact statements. Lead with the result, outcome or benefit to your employer. Here are a few examples of how to transform rough notes into accomplishment statements:

Position: Structural Engineer

Rough Notes: Questions that were asked of the engineer for his resume: Identify and describe your accomplishments in this position or identify and describe any accomplishments that address this topic:

Answered Comments:
- *Assigned as lead engineer / project manager for several of the company's high profile projects:*
- *850,000 sq. ft. warehouse and manufacturing facility for Fortune 500 Company.*
  - *Facility consists of perimeter concrete tilt-up panels.*
  - *Lateral resisting elements consist of concrete shear walls, special concentric brace frames (SCBF).*
- *1,200,000 sq. ft. warehouse and fulfillment facility for Fortune 500 Company.*
  - *Facility consists of perimeter concrete tilt-up panels.*
  - *Facility features two main mezzanines:*
    - *Single story concrete metal deck mezzanine with special moment resisting frames (SMRF) and special concentric brace frames (SCBF) as its lateral resisting elements.*
    - *Three story concrete metal deck mezzanine with SCBF as its lateral resisting elements.*
- *Manufacturing / office facility for Fortune 500 Company.*
  - *Headquarter for Fortune 500 Company intended for manufacturing, office use, and training.*

- *Facility houses overhead cranes and jib cranes within the manufacturing sector.*

Accomplishment Statement Sample: Accomplished and assigned to numerous high profile corporate projects for: Fortune 500 company and Fortune 500 company. Developed and derived additional designs for Fortune 500: single story concrete metal deck mezzanine with special moment resisting frames (SMRF) and special concentric brace frames (SCBF) as its lateral resisting elements and three story concrete metal deck mezzanine with SCBF as its lateral resisting elements and Fortune 500 Company that include: headquarters intended for manufacturing, office use, and training, as well as facility houses for overhead and jib cranes within this manufacturing sector.

Position: Real Estate Professional Manager

Rough Notes: Seeking employment for a sales/managerial position in real estate, risk management, finance, oil and gas, investment consultation.

Accomplishments Statement Sample: Served in a succession of increasingly responsible positions in real estate, risk management, finance, oil and gas, and investment consultation businesses in state name and the major metropolitan city areas.

Position: Administrative Assistant

Rough Notes: I have a highly developed sense of organization, sense of time management, and leadership skills.

Accomplishments Statement Sample: Expertise in Administration and Office Management; strengthened sense of organization, time management, and leadership skills.

Maybe you're Still Stuck?

It can be challenging to identify your accomplishments. Try asking your manager or a colleague to cite your major talents and contributions to the team - others may have an easier time recognizing your value than you. Review your job performance evaluations or reference letters, because usually they include your detailed accomplishments. Just don't sell yourself short by taking your accomplishments for granted. Potential employers see past success as an indicator of future performance. Your job search will be most effective as your resume showcases your key abilities or attainments.

Chapter 7
What's the Sixth Secret Step?

The sixth secret step is the best formatting for your Professional Experience section.

The Professional Experience or Work Section is the place for detailing your previous employment information. This section can be called Work Experience, Work History, Employment History, Employment Experience, Relevant Experience or whatever else indicates the type of information that is included. For instance, if you have strong volunteer experience in the field to which you are applying, you may want to title this section Relevant Experience rather than Employment Experience, in order to accurately represent the information.

What to Include in the Professional Experience Section?

This section should include most of the following:

- The names of the companies you worked for
- The city and state for each company
- The titles/positions you held
- Your employment dates for each job
- The duties you performed

This section should also include promotions you received while on each job, especially if they're relevant to the job title you are seeking. If you've had many promotions and/or titles with the same employer simply cite your first and last job titles to reflect your work accomplishments.

Citing your most accredited and measured successes is the most significant part of the Professional Experience Section. Your descriptive statements must be not only accurate and concise but should highlight duties that are most relevant to the position you seek. While it is acceptable to write full sentences in paragraph form for each position you held, it is also common to create a bulleted list of the duties you performed. See the resume samples on pages 64-66.

In creating your bulleted list, each bullet must be formatted in parallel form (which means that each item must be grammatically formatted the same). It is also a good idea that you put each item in the active voice and use powerful action verbs (see the Alphabetical Action Verb List, page 37). Each work experience should have at least three bulleted items with the most relevant duties listed first. Spend some time to considering what you actually accomplished for the job, list the specific activities and duties that you were responsible for, and craft poignant and concise descriptions representing those activities.

The following examples are illustrations that you can model:

Project Management Executive

- Dynamic, Product Management Professional with more than ten years' experience in execution of project-oriented work.
- Able to assure project objective adherence in combination with client expectations for time and cost.
- Outstanding success in motivating and launching products for Boeing Corporation.

How to Format the Professional Work Experience Section?

See the *A Killer Resume:* samples to peruse various formatting options, listed in the final chapters of this book.

Because each person's work history is unique, you may have unusual circumstances to represent on your résumé.

You might consider inputting the company name in a left-hand column, the city and state right after or perhaps in a center column, and entering your employment dates in a right-hand column. Remember, if you used columns in any other section of your resume document, you should make sure that they are a visual complement to the columns or section alignment that you use in the Work Experience section.

Formatting is crucial for the Professional Experience or Work History Sections because you are communicating a great deal of information very quickly and most concisely. You may want to consider one of the resume sample formats in the back Appendix of the book for a resume format.

What are Some Resume Writing Tips on Handling
Different Types of Work Experience?

If you have worked for an organization for many years
and held several ongoing positions, you can list each one
separately. If you are applying for a job outside of the
area that most of your work experience is in, you can
also include or list your relevant community service or
volunteer experience. If this is the case, you might also
want to consider a functional or skills resume, in which
you group several bulleted items by skills and abilities
rather than by each company or job. See our functional
resume example below for more details.

What Should a Student Resume Include?

If you are a student, or a recent graduate your resume
might contain summer or part time employment that is
not relevant to the position for which you are applying. If
this is your situation, just remember that you developed
skills in each position you have held. Be creative and
resourceful in creating these lists. For example, if you
worked at Burger King, you learned how to do the
following:

- Functioned succinctly in a group or team
  environment.
- Worked responsibly in an organized and time-
  sensitive environment.
- Sustained flexibility of duties from each work
  shift completed.

As your professional work experience pertains to your
field, you should drop off the oldest part time or summer
employment positions, relevant internships or

professional training programs until all of your listed work experience is relevant to your field.

It can be challenging to determine how to represent periods of unemployment. Consider listing other types of relevant work of what you were doing during that time period. For example, if you took time off work to raise your children, you can put volunteer or community service related work you may have done on your resume and detail what you accomplished.

If you took any classes (even if you did not obtain a degree), or attended training programs or completed appropriate certifications of study, i.e., programming classes in HTML, CSS, etc., or completed some Graphic Design program trainings where you learned Adobe Creative Suites, InDesign, Illustrator or Photoshop.

Perhaps you did some online classes or completed program study through video training like the well-respected Lynda.com training website or the digital marketing MarketMotive.com. Seek out your local community college counselor or perhaps your local university may have an extension or online program as well where such classes may be studied and cited during periods of non-work. You can list the educational activities you were involved in during that time.

Should My Resume be One or Two Pages or More?

Here's How to Determine Resume Length

Presently the job market is quite competitive - you may need to shorten a resume to one page to combat against age discrimination or to lengthen a resume to use multiple pages to persuade a potential employer to grant you an interview. Everyone's situation is unique. Remember you only need to list 10 years' experience, or, in some cases, only seven or eight years. Investigate who's competing for the jobs you seek by reading industry blogs (Problogger.net), marketplace blogs (MediaBistro.com) or reviewing group discussions on LinkedIn or other job seeking websites.

For resumes, limiting your document to one page is a good approach for industry specific resumes in fields like Accounting, Banking, Web Design or even for new college graduates and high school students. Don't feel cornered into one page - go ahead and add that extra page of accomplishments, as long as it is relevant and persuasive.

The following sections will give you more advice about when to use resumes of different lengths and will suggest ways to create a memorable second page. A third page may be used for curricula vitae (CVs), which are typically indicative of teachers, researchers and professional medical and legal fields.

Some specialized resumes may be three pages or longer if you are transitioning from a military career to a government job; USAA.com is a government job website that exiting soldiers use to search for jobs and others interested in a government job might use. Both military and government resumes require a great deal more of depth and personal information for each job experience cited. These resumes also require the applicant's entire work history, not just the last seven to 10 years.

Remember, though, that the length of your resume depends on the rhetorical situation and your audiences' needs.

When Should I Use One-Page Resumes?

A. New college graduates and other entry-level job seekers usually only need a single page resume for the following reasons:

1) The applicant does not have enough relevant experience to fill one page or more.
2) The situation requires the resume to focus on completed coursework and/or other field related leadership activities that connect you to the job you seek.
3) The resume is written to satisfy a job fair's expectations
4) The resume is created to meet a potential employer's expectations.

B. If you have less than ten years of experience, you may need to focus on one or two jobs, which may in turn shorten your resume to a single page.

1) Focus on your obtained skills.
2) It is not necessary to repeat every single action of that job to take up space; emphasize the relevant duties in measurable accomplishments.

C. If you are pursuing a minor or substantial career change, much of your experience may not be relevant to the new job.

1) Focus on your relevant skills obtained.
2) Do not grossly stretch your information to cover more than single page if you cannot

relate the work experience to your current
career goal in some way.

When Should You Use Two-Page Resumes?

A. Obviously, some recent college graduates and
other entry-level job seekers do have the
experience to qualify for a two-page resume
because of the following reasons:

1) Some employers require a second and
separate page for references.
2) The length of the document is extended due
to relevant jobs, internships, extracurricular
involvement, and leadership activities.
3) Try not to reduce your font to a size smaller
than 10 point or your margins less than one
inch. If you must do this to fit your work
experience on a one-page resume, then
consider extending to a two-page format.
4) Remember that recruiters at job fairs will
accept a two-page resume, but you can also
bring a one-page version to be safe.

B. Consider a two-page resume if you are above
entry-level experienced positions, but below the
executive level.

1) Always include the relevant various jobs you
have held.
2) Always include the relevant duties you have
held.

C. If you are seeking a job that requires technical or engineering or scientific skills, you may need a second page to your resume.

   1) You should list your relevant experience in technical, scientific or engineering fields.
   2) Listing your technical, engineering or scientific knowledge proves your abilities for the job you seek.

When Should Your Resume Length Exceed Two Pages?

A. If you are an experienced manager or a senior-level executive, your resume may require three or more pages.

   1) Your resume should include a long record of measureable leadership accomplishments.
   2) You may be required to give exact details of your past duties/responsibilities because you will be given more high-level task for the job you seek.
   3) You should include examples of your vision, flexibility, ethics, integrity, etc., because of the status of the position you are applying for.

B. If you are seeking a job in the academic or scientific field, you will likely be required to provide a curricula vita (a long resume, as described above, with possible citations of research or published work information). So, in addition to listing your education, you should include the following:

   1) Publications, presentations, licenses, etc.
   2) Teaching and/or research experience.

What Kind of Tips Can You Suggest for a Second or a Third Page?

Before you lengthen your resume longer, consider the position you seek and whether the additional experience on the resume will add to your viability for the position. If you should include that additional experience, then you should plan the extra pages. For instance, you may want to focus the extra page on key projects or senior level leadership skills. Perhaps this page should be titled to reflect its focus. For example, you may list or describe projects from classes, enhanced learning or certificated programs or graduate school. You could even include activities for honors sororities or fraternities.

You may find that the extra pages work best as supplemental sheets. Such sheets could list the aforementioned presentations, awards or technical skills. If you utilize this suggestion, perhaps pick or choose which extra pages should be sent to which employer. For example, you may forward the detailed list of technical skills to a computer company, but send the list of your research awards and presentations to a research firm.

When you include extra pages, you must consider the effect a longer resume will have on your recruiter and/or hiring manage. Therefore, you should always have the attention-getting information on the first page. Some employers may skip over the other pages altogether.

Coherence is also important for someone to understand your skills. You may need to avoid splitting the job details from one page to the next. You may, however, have one job detailed at the bottom of your resume's first page and another work experience description at the top of page two. The best way to increase coherency is to number the resume pages, you can include headers or footers, such as "Riley Rose's Accomplishments Continued…" In addition, consider adding a summary of your skills or keywords to the beginning of the resume. This is normally a part of the Qualifications Summary. The Keywords section should allow your readers to see your main qualifications at a glance…and then read the rest of your resume document to find more specific details.

To summarize, extra pages may:

- Focus on leadership skills or special educational projects.
- Work as supplemental pages to list detailed points of experience that specific (mostly senior level) audiences would want to know.

The additional pages past page two should also:

- Be coherent and organized
- Not lose your reader's interest

How to Write Each Section of Your Resume?

Carefully Enter Your Work Experience

Your work experience is one of the most important things an employer looks for on your resume. Enter this information carefully. Using the following suggestions to make the best impression, even if you have a less-than-perfect work history.

Choose the resume format you want: chronological, functional, or a combination. Input the dates, job titles, employer names, cities, and states of your work history in a resume format or template.

Chronological Resume

In the chronological and or combination format, your work experience will be typed in the body of the resume and later you will write achievement statements into bullet points for each job title.

Functional Resume

In the functional format, your work history is placed near the end of the resume very purposefully.

Both Chronological and Functional Resumes

In listing your work experience for both formats you should:

- List your jobs in reverse chronological order or your most recent employment first.
- Use years (no months) when listing dates on your resume. This makes it easier for the employer to quickly grasp your employment timeline.

How to Handle Work History Issues?

Most job applicants have a less-than-perfect work history, so you shouldn't worry if you have issues as well. What is most important is that you present your history so the resume reviewer doesn't notice or feels okay about your work history discrepancies.

What are the two frequent issues on resumes?

Unemployment is one frequent issue. If you've ever been laid off, fired, quit, or are returning to work after years of retirement, parenting, illness, or something else, make sure you don't leave those years blank in your stated work experience. Fill that gap with a relevant job title for some activity (paid or unpaid) that you were doing during that time. If you can't come up with a title that's relevant, then pick one that's honest and shows you have good character, such as parent or student. If it's left blank, an employer may think something bad happened that you don't want to talk about and you might not receive a call for an interview.

Do Dates on a Resume, Trigger Age Discrimination? Dates on your resume do give clues about your age. So be careful how far back in your history you go. Remember, you don't have to start with your first job if it's not to your advantage, you need only go back a maximum of ten years. What's important is that everything on your resume is accurate, so it's okay to leave early employment dates and the corresponding work history off of your resume. The goal is to find a job.

Once you've entered your work experience, you're ready for the next step towards completion of your resume: Awards, Achievements and Accreditations.

Chronological Resume Template

The chronological resume as described above in How to Choose a Resume Format is most preferred by recruiters and employers. It's especially attractive for job seekers who desire to stay in the same line of work and at the same level of employment. It's also a good layout for someone who wants to move up the corporate ladder in the line of work they're currently in.

Actually this resume format can handle some tough work history problems such as spans of unemployment, short-term jobs and age issues. It takes some thought to come up with solutions for such concerns, but it's worth your time to do so, since this format is well received by resume screeners and hiring managers.

Functional Resume Template

The functional resume format as described in How to Choose a Resume Format is the least preferred format by recruiters and employers. But, if you're making a minor or extreme career change or have a confusing or troubled work history, the functional resume format may be best for you. Just because it's not usually preferred, doesn't mean a well written and presented one won't get reviewed. It will.

See Sample Function Resume Template in Resume Samples Section included at the back of this book.

Combination Resume Template

The combination resume (as described in Choose a Resume Format) is very well received by recruiters and employers. It's a great resume format for career changers and for those seeking promotions or vertical career moves.

It's also a very good format for someone who needs to give meaning to hard-to-understand job titles. This is sometimes the case with government, military and college job titles that use numbers or codes to show what level they are. As you can see in the combination resume template below the skills headings help explain the job title.

Combination Resume Template

See the attached Combination Resume Template in the Section of Resume Samples at the end of this book for reference.

The following resume template is an image that you can view to grasp how the combination resume is structured.

If you'd like to download a combination resume template, please see my Ready-Made Resumes program. The templates are in Word and come in many graphic layouts.

Combination Resume Sample Below:

FIRST A. LAST

XXXX XXth Avenue ~ CITY, STATE Zip code

333-444-5555   email@emailaddress.com

PROJECT MANAGEMENT EXECUTIVE

Quantitative Structures ~ Information Technology ~ Business Analysis

QUALIFICATIONS SUMMARY

Dynamic, Product Management Professional with more than ten years experience in execution of project-oriented work. Able to assure project objective adherence in combination with client expectations for time and cost. Outstanding success in motivating and launching products for Fortune 500 Corporation. Upbeat, active practitioner, results-oriented, with a collaborative and persuasive management style. Excellent quantitative skills combining expertise in business applications, systems technology, and communications. Strong analytical, organizational, and diverse management skills. Knowledge of multiple service platforms. Excels in a fast paced environment with demonstrative quick learning. Additional abilities in:

♦ Program Management	♦ Communications	♦ Budget Analysis
♦ Problem Resolution	♦ Business Planning	♦ Sales and Marketing
♦ Quality Assurance	♦ Administrative Support	♦ Cost Benefit Analysis

CAREER ACCOMPLISHMENTS

FORTUNE 500 COMPANY

- Directed large volume activities for multiple mediums and operational systems environments.
- Coordinated the set-up of varied quality assurance and project communications for cross-functional, corporate marketing efforts.
- Completed Fortune 500 Company Corporation Management Training incorporating priority project ranking, staff coaching, personnel counseling, team collaboration, facilitated adherence in the midst of ethics' challenges and administered business process management tactics.

FORTUNE 500 COMPANY

- Sited for Relationship Selling Skills and Information Technology adherence standards while at FORTUNE 500 COMPANY.
- Worked directly with senior management to identify and prioritize opportunities and analyze risks associated with assigned projects.
- Supported senior leadership by project status reports and performance standard results.
- Facilitated and contributed to consultant hiring as well as overseeing project activities.
- Mentored Project Managers of varied grades to ensure development and application of necessary skills and knowledge in order to meet client expectations.
- Managed numerous projects simultaneously and collaboratively worked with team members as assigned.
- Guided group assessments effectively and purposefully managed working project group dynamics to foster team building and achieve meeting objectives.

PROFESSIONAL EXPERIENCE

Project Management

- Exceptional leadership demonstrated by management of First Forms Audit in support of salient business unit.
- Directed inventory fulfillment, testing adherence, and implementation of quality assurance for Fortune 500 Company electronic forms management software system.
- Organized workshops consisting of 120 members of staff personnel, for purposes of tracking mechanisms and reporting on dispersed team members inclusive of senior management.
- Accomplished improved interdepartmental information processing and decreased paper related expenses by $2.4 million within 9 months.
- Managed by breaking projects down into time-phases and measurable milestones.
- Ensured that diverse, cross-functional activities produced a pre-determined result within known cost and scheduled constraints.
- Identified appropriate people, facilities, tools and materials, vendors, etc. for accomplished end goals.
- Considered potential costs and benefits of resources prior to allocating them.
- Balanced time and resources effectively.

Business Planning

- Created strong cross-functional collaborative working relationships with geographically dispersed parties for improved project deadlines, surpassing departmental goal by 11%.
- Utilized advanced coaching skills to improve work and reinforce performance of teammates.
- Facilitated skill development by providing clear, behaviorally specific feedback, additionally made specific suggestions for improvement in a manner that built group confidence while maintaining self-esteem.

Technical Applications and Communications

- Appointed liaison with users, suppliers and Procurement to establish standards, addressed modification requests, and performed product tests before releasing improvements to external users.
- Accomplished exceptionally high level of customer satisfaction and improved company image by measured proportions.
- Communicated ideas with clear and effective expression, thoughts, and concepts in both verbal and written and/or graphic forms.
- Utilized appropriate communication skills for concise presentations incorporated multi media and technical abilities; with the intent of immediate impact.
- Demonstrated wide knowledge and ability in one or more areas of technical expertise - marketing, finance, information technology, human resources, fundraising - fully credible and widely respected for technical know-how.
- Understood and applied standard information technology project management tools and methodologies in management of IT projects.

WORK HISTORY

FORTUNE 500, City, STATE, *Communication Liaison*   2004 – Present
FORTUNE 500, City, STATE, *Project Manager*   2001 – 2004

EDUCATION

UNIVERSITY OR COLLEGE NAME, City, STATE
Masters of Business Administration, GRADUATION YEAR (optional)

UNIVERSITY OR COLLEGE NAME, City, STATE
Bachelor of Science in Marketing, GRADUATION YEAR (optional)

Pick the correct resume format for you and write the best professional resume you can.

Chapter 8
What's the Seventh Secret Step?

The seventh secret step is the Education & Training section and the Affiliations, Awards & Accreditations section. Affiliations, Awards & Accreditations section is an excellent section to display your professional uniqueness and why you are distinct from the many submitting, distinguishing your resume as *a killer*. Remember the *killer resume* is always professional. It may be unique and distinct but it is also professional.

When you are writing a resume, the education section of your resume should include your educational background. In this section of your resume, list the schools you attended, the degrees you attained, and any special awards and honors you earned.

Professional development courses and certifications should also be included in this section of your resume.

A Resume Education Section Sample Includes:

- College, Degree, Graduation Date – optional

- Awards, Honors

- Certifications

- Professional Development Courses

Resume Education Section Example:

University of California, Los Angeles
Bachelor of Arts in English, May 2012 – *date is optional*
Department Honors

Accounting Certification
March 2009

Again, if you have been in the workforce for several years, you don't need to include the date you graduated.

If you are not sure how to list the college coursework you have accumulated on your resume if you didn't finish your degree, below are a few options that will let employers know you have accumulated some credits, even though you didn't complete college graduation.

1. List the name of your college, the location, the number of credits completed and optionally, the years attended:

A. Loyola Marymount College, Los Angeles, California, 2010-12, completed 48 credits

or

B. Loyola Marymount College
Los Angeles, California

You can also mention the focus of your studies if it is related to your employment objective and the number of credits completed in that discipline i.e. completed 48 credits, including 24 credits in business.

> 2. Another option for the coursework that is related to your career objective, is to list some of that coursework that is related to the job for which you are applying. For example:

>> A. Related Coursework:
>> Accounting 101 and 102, Business Management, Marketing, Finance and Statistics.

> 3. Yet another possibility is to actually describe in summary detail, any courses or related projects to your target job. Consider this approach if your work experience that is relevant to the position you seek, is thin.

>> A. For example, a person who is aiming for a job in IT or Information Technology might describe a project directly related to the specific programming experience desired in the job description for which they are seeking.

High School Equivalency Tests

High school equivalency tests are for individuals who haven't graduated from high school. They can take the General Educational Development (or GED) test, which is a high school equivalency exam and intern receive a GED diploma or certificate. The GED credential, certifies the individual passing this test to have the equivalent knowledge and skills to a high school graduate.

List your GED on your resume and job applications, just as you would list a high school diploma or if you had attended college, other classes and/or continuing education courses.

In addition, there are some states that have their own equivalency exams. California is one of these states. It offers the California High School Proficiency Exam (CHSPE). This exam is for high school students living in California who wish to leave high school early. Thus, students who pass the CHSPE exam receive a Certificate of Proficiency from the State of California. A CHSPE degree is the legal equivalent to a California high school diploma.

Remember to list your high school equivalency certificate or diploma you obtain on your resume in the Education & Training section exactly as you would list your high school diploma.

How should you list your GED on your resume and job applications?

Once you've completed college or are in the midst of studying for your college Bachelors degree after obtaining your GED, there is no need to list your GED on your resume. You only need to include your college education in the Education & Training section of your resume.

If there is no continuing education or acquired work experience that you can include on your resume, then do list your GED in the Education & Training section.

Samples of how to list your GED certificate on your resume are sited below:

> A. Education & Training
> - General Educational Development Certificate, year – *again listing the year is optional*

What If You Are Working on a GED?

If you are still working on the GED, but haven't obtained your certificate or diploma, you can list your GED with your intended graduation date, this shows that you are currently studying towards obtaining it:

> B. Education & Training
> - General Educational Development Diploma, May 2014 – *you can list the intended month and date of graduation*

> or

> C. Education & Training
> - General Educational Development Diploma, Actively Enrolled

Here's how to list a California Certificate of Proficiency on your resume:

> D. Education & Training
> - CHSPE Certificate (Certificate of Proficiency from the State of California)

The Value of a GED

Why makes obtaining a GED significant if you haven't completed your high school graduation? A GED is your equivalent to a high school diploma. Most employers desire job seekers who have a minimum education level that is equivalent to a high school level graduate. Thus, a GED is a qualified legal certification to a high school diploma, even for entry-level positions.

Additionally, apprenticeship programs seek apprentices who have high school level education in order to be considered for their programs. Both Universities and colleges seek applicants that have their GED or a high school graduate diploma.

Without a GED or high school diploma, it will be difficult to job search. It's especially hard when unemployment is high and there is a lot of competition for available jobs.

GED vs. High School Diploma

The American Council on Education states that almost 96 percent of employers in the United States do accept a GED credential identically to a high school graduate's diploma. In fact, most private and government industry employers in addition to university and college level admissions offices approve a GED certification just as they would a high school level graduate's diploma.

Thus, it is very important to include your GED certification on your resume even if you didn't attend college or a university. You are demonstrating to an employer that you possess the same qualified documents as a high school graduate.

Conclusion

Write the best professional resume you can for each job title you apply for. Each resume you write should be targeted specifically to the job you seek. It's comprehensive and tedious work. It's the distinctiveness of your resume or personal branding that will shine in the eyes of the resume screener and the hiring manager looking to fill the job advertised.

Remember, being distinctive or unique will help you to stand out from the masses (with your *killer resume*), like the candidate that had alligator wresting under special interests. I know of a graphic designer who designed her own logo for her stationery, resume and website. It helped distinguish her and because her designs were tasteful yet still complementary, it caught the attention of the hiring manager. So stand out distinctively from the pack and make your special skills call the attention of the gatekeeper.

Remember while both content and layout are important, content is the most significant. Content is the distinction that makes your resume *a killer.*

Included in *A Killer Resume* are several resume templates. You can find many on the Internet for free, in fact. Choose

a nice professional layout appropriate to your industry
- be it business, information technology or graphic design.
However the content of your resume is what will get you
hired. This book is written so you can easily grasp what
needs to be included so you are presented in the most
accomplished manner. Yet it contains everything the
gatekeeper and the hiring manager is looking for so that
you secure an interview, leading to the job you are
searching for.

If it's challenging to compose and write your very own
resume, that's actually a very good sign that you're on
the right path. Get a good friend who's talented at
reading and editing so you feel confident that you're
submitting the best resume possible. It's always within
your discretion to hire a professional resume writer if
you're not convinced the resume you crafted falls short
of your expectations.

To summarize, remember a resume objective is outdated
and nonspecific to the particular job you want. A
Qualifications Summary should be utilized instead of an
Objective Statement.

Versatility is also key. As you write each of your
resumes for the different jobs you seek, take note of
the tone of the job description - it will aid in your
communication of fitting into the professional career
world you desire.

Read and apply the seven secret steps to writing your
professional resume and you will have the marketing tool
you want for your new professional resume.

Remember your well-written resume is the ticket to the job
you desperately want. It's your marketing strategy to nail

down the career you have targeted and when you land it, it's a wonderful goal to have met.

Seven Step Summary
1) Job Description
   A resume begins with determining the job you want. Your resume is your most powerful marketing element. You must write it to target the exact job description you are applying for. Job descriptions are like cooking by a recipe to prepare your favorite meal. They are your road map to designing your best personal brand.

2) Resume Headline
   The second secret step is a resume headline. The headline of the resume should correspond to the job description title that you are applying for. Make sure you are qualified to fulfill this responsibility - why else would you be applying for this position unless you can competently do the work? Remember you are making these choices because you are applying to be chosen because your skills match the job description requirements.

   This is the first attention-grabbing element of your most important marketing tool, your resume. The resume headlines are several expressive statements that briefly and creatively highlight key skills and accomplishments throughout your career. These few statements must capture the reader's attention.

   The heading or title of a job description is the job title that an applicant should target. Examples include the following: Senior IT Project Manager, Vice President of Insurance, Management Consultant, Head Teacher, etc. A resume headline offers a job seeker the opportunity to shine. A well-formed headline will get your resume placed on top of the pile not stuffed somewhere in the middle.

Here are some good resume headline samples that you can personalize according to your needs:

- Marketing Campaign Manager
- Corporate Communications Professional
- Professional Account Executive
- Director of Sales
- Sales Manager
- Interior Designer
- Business Developer Professional
- Software Developer
- Research & Development Team Leader

3) Qualifications Summary
   Professional resumes should contain a summary statement and not a job objective. A statement tells what qualifies you to fill the job description you are applying for versus a career objective, which tells an employer what you're looking for.

   A profile is a very condensed version of a cover letter. A resume profile is a career summary or personal profile statement, compiled into a summary of qualifications. It profiles your key qualifications for the job you seek.

4) Keywords
   Resume keywords are the words that gatekeepers and/or hiring managers search for in their new database of resumes. In order for your resume to

be found, it needs to contain keywords that directly target the job description you are applying for.

Your resume's keywords should include the specific job descriptions you are applying for as well as your skills, software and technology competencies, relevant credentials and previous employers. These should be utilized throughout your resume but definitely in the Qualifications Summary of your resume.

Keywords are one to two word descriptors and/or adjectives that identify your areas of work expertise. A keyword section is included beneath the statement of qualifications. The keyword section is derived from this candidate's job skills.

For example, based on experience, a candidate for an employee change management position might use the following resume keywords: human resource ethics, recruitment and retention, legal expert and risk and cost analysis. A customer service account executive could include: lead conversion, client tracking system, Microsoft Office computer skills and perhaps order entry experience.

The best way to locate keywords for your resume is to utilize a job search engine like: Monster, CareerBuilder or Indeed (there are many) to search for job listings with. Review the results to find common keywords listed in the job postings. Incorporate those into your resume. Also check the list for action keywords you can use to describe your skills.

Remember to also include more of the job description keywords to describe your skills in your cover letter to increase your chances of getting selected for an interview.
This way, if your cover letter is screened, you will have a better chance of getting selected for an interview as a qualified candidate.

See the alphabetical listing of suggested keywords in Chapter 5, which is devoted to keyword selection.

5) Career Accomplishments
The fifth secret step is a section on Career Accomplishments. Dig deep for resume accomplishments, these are critical and distinctive as discussed earlier in outside interests for your reference.

What is the Definition of an Accomplishment?

For your resume, an accomplishment is a description or an example of how you contributed toward your job. It's an achievement that states or describes the type of worker you are. The best employer accomplishments are measurable. See examples 1, 2 and 3 below:

1). A studio tax manager conveys her hands-on accounting prowess: "Reviews divisional submission for quarterly and year-end tax provision; directs and coordinates varying domestic operations projects and assists with inquiries from taxing authorities."

2). A recent college graduate describes her work at a major retail store, training new hires on how to operate a cash register for shoppers during their purchase checkout: "Trains new employees on the POS registers with 100% efficiency and less than a 2% error rating."

3). A structural engineer describes his work for an architectural design firm: "Filled in as a structural drafter when necessary, generated and revised structural details and originated structural plans, elevations and sections."

If you still need help identifying your accomplishments, see the 10-minute exercise in Chapter 6 to help you do so.

6) Professional Experience
The sixth secret step is the best formatting for your Professional Experience section. The Professional Experience or Work Section is the place for detailing your previous employment information. This section can be called Work Experience, Work History, Employment History, Employment Experience, Relevant Experience, or whatever else indicates the type of information that is included.

What to Include in the Professional Experience Section?

This section should include most of the following:

- The names of the companies you worked for.
- The city and state for each company.

- The titles/positions you held.
- Your employment dates for each job.
- The duties you performed.

While it is acceptable to write full sentences in paragraph form for each position you held, it is also common to create a bulleted list of the duties you performed. See the resume samples on pages 64-66.

In creating your bulleted list, each bullet must be formatted in parallel form (which means that each item must be grammatically formatted the same). It is also a good idea that you put each item in the active voice and use powerful action verbs (see the Alphabetical Action Verb List). Each work experience should have at least three bulleted items with the most relevant duties listed first. Spend some time considering what you actually accomplished for the job, list the specific activities and duties that you were responsible for and craft poignant and concise descriptions representing those activities.

If you are applying for a job outside of the area that most of your work experience is in, you can also include or list your relevant community service or volunteer experience. If this is the case, you might also want to consider a Functional or Skills Resume, in which you group several bulleted items by skills and abilities rather than by each company or job. See our Functional Resume example below for more details.

What Should a Student Resume Include?

If you are a student, or a recent graduate your resume might contain summer or part time employment that is not relevant to the position for which you are applying. If this is your situation, just remember that you developed skills in each position you have held. Be creative and resourceful in creating these lists. For example, if you worked at Burger King, you learned how to do the following:

- Functioned succinctly in a group or team environment.
- Worked responsibly in an organized and time-sensitive environment.
- Sustained flexibility of duties from each work shift completed.

As your professional work experience pertains to your field, you should drop off the oldest part time or summer employment positions, relevant internships or professional training programs until all of your listed work experience is relevant to your field.

It can be challenging to determine how to represent periods of unemployment. Consider listing other types of relevant work of what you were doing during that time period, such as volunteer work or pertinent classes or training.

Should My Resume be One or Two Pages or More?

Here's How to Determine Resume Length

Presently the job market is quite competitive - you may need to shorten a resume to one page to combat against age discrimination or to lengthen a resume to use multiple pages to persuade a potential employer to grant you an interview. Everyone's situation is unique. Remember you only need list 10 years' experience, and, in some cases, only seven or eight years. Investigate who's competing for the jobs you seek by reading industry blogs (Problogger.net), marketplace blogs (MediaBistro.com) or reviewing group discussions on LinkedIn or other job seeking websites.

For resumes, limiting your document to one page is a good approach for industry specific resumes in fields like Accounting, Banking, Web Design or even new college graduates and high school students. Don't feel cornered into one page, go ahead and add that extra page of accomplishments, as long as it is relevant and persuasive.

A third page may be used for curricula vitae (CVs), which are typically indicative of teachers, researchers and professional medical and legal fields.

Some specialized resumes may be three pages or longer if you are transitioning from a military career to a government job (USAA.com is a government job website that exiting soldiers use to search for jobs and others interested in a government job might use). Both military and government resumes require a great deal more in depth each job experience and also requires the applicant's entire work history, not just the past 7 – 10 years.

Remember, though, that the length of your resume depends on the rhetorical situation and your audiences' needs. Also choose the resume format you want: chronological, functional, or a combination. Input the dates, job titles, employer names, cities, and states of your work history in a resume format or template.

See Chapter 6 on specific resume types (chronological, functional or a combination) and examples of when to use one page, two pages or more lengthy resume versions, like a curriculum vitae.

7) Education & Training section and Affiliations, Awards & Accreditations section.

The seventh secret step is the Education & Training section and the Affiliations, Awards & Accreditations section.

When you're writing a resume, the education section of your resume should include your educational background. In this section of your resume, list the schools you attended, the degrees you attained, and any special awards and honors you earned.

Professional development courses and certifications should also be included in this section of your resume.

A Resume Education Section Sample Includes:

- College, Degree, Graduation Date – optional

- Awards, Honors

- Certifications

- Professional Development Courses

Resume Education Section Example:

University of California, Los Angeles
Bachelor of Arts in English, May 2012 – *date is optional*
Department Honors

Accounting Certification
March 2009

Again, if you have been in the workforce for several years, you don't need to include the date you graduated.

If you are not sure how to list the college coursework you have accumulated on your resume if you didn't finish your degree, below are a few options that will let employers know you have accumulated some credits, even though you didn't complete college graduation.

1. List the name of your college, the location, the number of credits completed and optionally, the years attended:

A. Loyola Marymount College, Los Angeles, California, 2010-12, completed 48 credits

or

B. Loyola Marymount College
Los Angeles, California

Crafting a strong resume means drawing together the professional events and accomplishments that creatively and succinctly tell your professional story. Take the time necessary to complete your best resume and utilize your most comprehensive resources to put together the best resume possible with each job you apply for and always remember to include something unique and distinctive to separate you from the pack of applicants. Remember your individuality is what makes you special, do your best to communicate this in your most vital marketing component, your resume.

Best wishes in your search endeavors. Thank you for reading this book and utilizing your best endeavors to write your very best professional resume.

Appendix

Resume Samples – see attached

Education/Sports Professional Resume

Xxxx X. Xxxxxx
(XXX) XXX-XXXX ext. XXX ~ email@email.com

Street Address ~ City, State, Zip code

QUALIFICATIONS

Noted Collegiate Professional encompassing Media and Public Relations. Focused experience and education in marketing, public relations, and sports business. Various accomplishments inclusive of the WBCA National Convention, All-Star Challenge, and High School All-America Game Awards for Women's Basketball Coaches Association in Lilburn, Georgia. Superior communication skills, easily interacts with executives, sports agencies, clients, vendors and corresponding staff. Golden Key International Honor Society Member and a Snider Scholar.

PROFESSIONAL EXPERIENCE

WOMEN'S BASKETBALL COACHES ASSOCIATION, City, State   2005 – Present
Communications and Awards Intern

- Supports Communications department for the awards program specifically related to the WBCA National Convention, All-Star Challenge, and the High School All-America Game.
- Creates publicity materials for all WBCA publication of, "Coaching Women's Basketball" media, as well as prescribed press releases.
- Sets-up awards/election convention including: award distributions, winner response tracking and recipient travel arrangements.
- Collaborates with Multimedia Manager for on-site management of banquets inclusive of processional linguistics and list composition, cited recognition of head table attendees, and special moment award photography displaying special guests and recipients.
- Compiles bios for WBCA All-Star Challenge and High School All-America Game and convention's program, assembles headshots for speakers, as well as comprising press kit information for actual game events.
- Determines and sustains appropriate aspects of the Division II Coaches Poll.

CHELTENHAM HIGH SCHOOL, City, State   2000 – Present
Cheerleading Coach

- Administrates and officiates cheerleading squad for all required sporting and special event practice, training, and performances.
- Plans and constructs team budget, organizes annual team clinic and directs all team fundraising projects.

FREE LIBRARY OF PENNSYLVANIA, City, State   2002 – 2003
Design Studio Assistant

- Compiled, constructed, and re-drafted budget for resultant studio operations.
- Conceived and produced announcement media for library distribution of studio services.

Public Relations Intern

- Designed and organized the project, "Access Technology", specifically for the blind and visually impaired.
- Compiled media kit press releases, fact sheet/backgrounders', and public service announcements for "Access Technology" sponsored event.

Xxxx X. Xxxxxx

PHILADELPHIA FIGHT, City, State   2001
Publications Reactions/Special Events Intern

- ➤ Developed advertising strategies and special events planning for customer relationship management.
- ➤ Administered database combined with corporate proposals relevant to special broadcast operations and events.

LAMOTT COMMUNITY CENTER, City, State   2001
Intern

- ➤ Assisted Community Center Director with Fall planning and program implementations, fundraising logistics, and other special event and/or summer playground camp activities.

EDUCATION

COLLEGE OR UNIVERSITY, City, State
Bachelor of Science in Tourism and Hospitality Management with a specialization in Sport and Recreations Management, 2002

REFERENCES AVAILABLE UPON REQUEST

Student/Young Professional Resume

<u>*Xxxxx Xxxxx Xxxxxxxxx*</u>

Street Address, City, State Zip code (XXX) XXX-XXXX   email@email.com

Retail Management Professional with extensive experience in buying, merchandising, and store operations. Background includes various environments: consulting, small firms and large corporations. Areas of focus include all aspects of Marketing with a specialty in Advertising and Sales. Accomplished Trainer in Personnel Management.

• **Sales & Marketing**	• **Motivational Training**	• **Window Display & Design**
• **Product Branding & Development**	• **Strategic Planning**	• **Staff Coaching**

PROFESSIONAL EMPLOYMENT

2000 to Present   <u>**News Café Stores**</u>, City, State
DISTRICT MANAGER/BUYER
- Retail Shop Operations Supervisor and Primary Buyer.
- Tremendous travel conducted to identify new products and make new acquisitions.
- Completed personnel hires, staff trainings and scheduled personnel coverage.
- Attained double-digit sales growth during acquisition period.
- Signature logo design and branding package introductions.
- Key market segments identified.

1997 to 1999   <u>**Miamigo Magazine,**</u> City, State
OPERATIONS MANAGER
- Launched office startup from 3-person operation to 20-person publication with over 30,000 subscriptions.
- Managed operations for weekly South Beach lifestyle and fashion magazine.
- Extensive responsibilities: budgeting, campaigns & promotions, and partnership creation.

1995 to 1997   <u>**Area One Entertainment,**</u> City, State
GENERAL MANAGER
- Management of *"Swirl"* nightclub and restaurant.
- Marketing contribution directly responsible for club's prevalent success.
- Supervised and approved hiring, training, staff functions, and food & beverage.
- Set-up business permits/licenses, and internal regulatory code enforcement of class type A establishment.
- Administered over all expenses and attained high average dollars sales per square foot.

1994 to 1995   <u>**Two Boots Restaurant Group**</u>, City, State
DISTRICT MANAGER
- Manhattan chain restaurant management.
- Revenue $4 million per store.
- Overseer for all stock suppliers, orders and purchasing.
- Reconciled daily receipts and register totals.
- Hired and trained personnel.

1990 to 1993   <u>**Blockbuster Entertainment**</u>, City, State
TRAINING STORE MANAGER
- Development of management and associate customer service training programs.
- Trained new store managers in day-to day operations and standard processes.
- Generated store budgets, profit & loss statements, and inventory control systems.

1987 to 1990   <u>**Pottery Barn/Williams Sonoma**</u>, City, State
TRAINING STORE MANAGER
- Developed and conducted 8-week Store Management Program in Regional Training Office.
- Successfully implemented ongoing coaching and store management development.
- Administered and approved all Merchandising for store displays.

PROFESSIONAL ACCOMPLISHMENTS

- *Member of Miami Beach Community Advisory Development Board*: 1993 – 1998.
- *Operations Coordinator for Care Resource / Dade Human Rights Foundation Fundraiser*: *The Winter Party*, 1995 – 2000 encompassing Marketing, Fundraising and Education Campaign Activities.
- *Assistant Campaign Manager*: Miami Beach Mayor Campaign.

SKILLS

- *Design & implementation for Point of Sale/Retail Systems.*
- *AS 400, NCR, IBM, Retail Pro, Retail STAR, and Fujitsu.*
- *Microsoft Office Suite, Macintosh and PC Platform, Graphic Design.*
- *Conversant in Conversational Spanish.*

Senior Executive Professional

XXXX XXXXXXX, JD, CAE, SPHR

Street ~ City, State, Zip code

(310) 555-1212   email@email.com

SENIOR MANAGEMENT EXECUTIVE

Organizational Development ~ Compliance Leadership ~ Risk Management

Exceptional leadership demonstrated by managing large staffs in Fortune 500 and multi-million dollar corporations. Trusted presidential advisor of measurement and analysis on all corporate objectives. Extraordinary tactical insight demonstrated in all contract negotiations and corporate legal matters. Expert ability for staff inspired excellence through effective hands-on management and governing abilities. State Bar licensing in California, New York and Nevada. Member of the National Legal Committee for the American Association of Homes and Services for the Aged; Alumni Board of Directors, Stanford University; Alumna Leadership of Los Angeles Community Trust Association; American Bar Association Leader for the National Officer Law Division and House of Delegates Representative. Additional abilities in:

♦ Change Management	♦ Human Resource Ethics	♦ Risk & Cost Analysis
♦ Legal Expert	♦ Training & Development	♦ Business Development
♦ Six Figure Settlements	♦ Recruitment & Retention	♦ Strategic Alliances

PROFESSIONAL ACCOMPLISHMENTS

ASSOCIATION OF FUNDRAISING PROFESSIONALS – Donors Forum of California – Course Accreditation listing including prerequisite of five years work experience.
- (1) Planned Giving 101, (2) Planned Giving 102, (3) Proposal Writing, (4) Building Strategic Relationships with Corporations and Foundations, (5) Conducting a Successful Capital Campaign, (6) Defining and Measuring Success: Program Outcome Evaluation for Nonprofit Organizations, (7) Major Gifts Fundraising and (8) Seeking Support From Individuals

RADIO AND TELEVISION SPONSORED BROADCASTS – varied media events include:
- **National Conference – Legal Panel** – American Assoc. for Homes and Services for the Aging "*Conducting A Legal Audit of Your Co.*"
- **Designer and Talent for Radio & Television Recruitment Ads** – Pfizer Laboratories
- **Editor of Newsletter** – Pfizer Laboratories

CAREER ACCOMPLISHMENTS

TIMEMARK CORPORATION
- Exceptional legal prowess winning 100% of all cases since 1990. Additionally saved over $500,000 in legal fees from outside billings. Collected damages exceeding $700,000 in legal settlements. Handled over 150 cases per year including Administrative, State and Federal court matters.
- Created and oversaw cost reduction and revenue generation for corporate purchasing, conference management and office services. Designed and managed a $400,000 telecommunications project. Developed an improved dispute and collection resolution system for 3 nursing homes, encompassing 550 hospital beds and 2000 housing units.
- Directed 10 departments: Legal, Human Resources, Management Information Services, Corporate and Healthcare Purchasing, Risk Management, Training and Development, Conference Management Services, Office Services and Telecommunications.

PROFESSIONAL EXPERIENCE

TIMEMARK CORPORATION, City, State   1987 to 2001
General Counsel &Vice President of Support Services
- Directed over staffs of 12 to 100 for international health care provider. Administered $4 - 6 million in budgets including employee benefits program and purchasing volume for corporate, medical and non-medical supplies. Presided direction for 52 sites in 4 states and lead 6 Administration and Operation Departments.
- Designated leadership resulted in Environmental Services Staff at all 52 sites achieving consistently high ratings from local, state and federal inspections. Budget increased 300% from 1987 to 1990 and duties increased proportionately.

NEW YORK TRANSIT AUTHORITY, City, State   1984 to 1987
Director of Grievances and Arbitrations
- Developed an expeditious grievance resolution system and formulated an arbitration program.

NATIONAL LABOR RELATIONS BOARD, City, State   1981 to 1984
Staff Attorney
- Investigated, resolved and litigated unfair labor practice charges in addition to conduction of union elections in New York.

NEW YORK CITY CORPORATION COUNSEL OFFICE, City, State   1979 to 1981
Labor Law Attorney
- Demonstrated a significant role in collective bargaining, contract negotiations and mediations for the New York Police and Fire Departments.

NEW YORK INSTITUTE OF CONTINUING LEGAL EDUCATION, City, State   1980
Legal Instructor of Prominent New York Institute for Continuing Educational Instruction.
- Coordinated seminar for varied CLE seminars, instruction material published for continuing educational reference material.

BURTON III MANAGEMENT, City, State   1979 to 1983
Instructor of Seminars for American Management Association and the U.S. Office of Personnel Management.
- Developed topics of seminar instruction for the American Management Association and the U.S. Office of Personnel Management.

WASHINGTON POST, City, State   1975 to 1977
Systems Trainer
- Co-developed the mandatory five-week management development program for all managers.

PFIZER LABORATORIES, City, State   1972 to 1975
Personnel Administrator
- Directed the new Human Resource Information System for a Research & Development Distribution Center.

EDUCATION

UNIVERSITY OF CALIFORNIA, Los Angeles, California, *Juris Doctor*, 1978
CAPITOL UNIVERSITY, Washington, D.C., *Master of Science*, 1975
STANFORD UNIVERSITY, Stanford, California, *Bachelor of Arts/Urban Studies*, 1972

Visit http://www.AKillerResume.com to download the resume sample templates, above.

Thank you for reading *A Killer Resume*. Stay tuned for upcoming books on how to do A Killer Interview, write a Killer Cover Letter, a Killer Follow-up and a Thank You letter, too. Just remember to include the uniqueness of you in your *killer resume* so that you are the professional exception that stands out from the pact. You are distinctively you and remember to always communicate this in your *killer resume*.

The End.

www.ingramcontent.com/pod-product-compliance
Lightning Source LLC
Chambersburg PA
CBHW030912180526
45163CB00004B/1803